Charles Janeway Stillé

Northern Interests and Southern Independence

A Plea for United Action

Charles Janeway Stillé

Northern Interests and Southern Independence
A Plea for United Action

ISBN/EAN: 9783337001834

Printed in Europe, USA, Canada, Australia, Japan

Cover: Foto ©Suzi / pixelio.de

More available books at **www.hansebooks.com**

AND

SOUTHERN INDEPENDENCE:

A PLEA FOR UNITED ACTION.

BY

CHARLES J. STILLÉ.

mmes agissent, mais Dieu les mène.—BOSSUET.

PHILADELPHIA:

M S. & ALFRED MARTIEN,

606 CHESTNUT STREET.

1863.

NORTHERN INTERESTS

AND

SOUTHERN INDEPENDENCE:

A PLEA FOR UNITED ACTION.

BY

CHARLES J. STILLÉ.

Les hommes agissent, mais Dieu les mène.—BOSSUET.

PHILADELPHIA:

WILLIAM S. & ALFRED MARTIEN,

606 CHESTNUT STREET.

1863.

TO THE READER.

THE writer of the following pages proposes to examine the probable effect of Southern Independence upon some of the vital material interests of the North. He trusts that this examination, while it may illustrate the value of the Union, will also show the importance of united action among ourselves to secure its permanence. His earnest desire is to prove how intensely practical a thing American nationality is, and he will not hesitate to condemn, with equal frankness, the extreme views of either party, when they seem to him to conflict with its developement.

PHILADELPHIA, *February,* 1863.

WE have now reached a period in the progress of the war when the prospect before us, in one aspect at least, is clear and unmistakable. Many of us have been from the beginning groping our way through mists and darkness, uncertain where that way might lead us, and fondly hoping that the rising sunlight would dispel the dim phantom of ill-omen which had haunted our footsteps during our dreary journey. But alas! while that sunlight may have chased away the phantom, it has revealed in its place a monster of more "hideous mien," proclaiming in open and defiant tones the deliberate purpose of our enemies to establish on our borders an independent, foreign, and necessarily hostile power.

We confess that we have been long in coming to the belief that the southern people were in earnest in hoping to carry out a scheme so extraordinary. It seemed necessary to deny to them the possession of an ordinary share of good sense and common

foresight, to suppose that they could really expect
to establish permanently such a government, or that
they really believed that the people of the North
could by any possible combinations ever be made
to consent to it. This hesitation, which has been
shared by many, has unquestionably served much to
weaken the enthusiasm with which, otherwise, the
war would have been constantly supported. But
there can be room for doubt no longer. It would
be waste of time to examine all the declarations of
the rebels on this point, but from the course ma-
lignity of the Richmond newspapers, to the vulgar
mendacity of Mr. Davis's speech at Jackson, they
all agree in this,—that the inflexible purpose of the
leaders at the South is, to establish, if they can, a
great independent slave power on this continent,
and that to render such a power safe and strong,
every State which has the bad taste or the bad
policy to prohibit slavery within its borders, must
on that account be denied any participation in such
a government, and that any theory of reconstruction
or reconciliation, based on constitutional guarantees,
—even one which would secure the services of the
whole population of the North as slaves, according
to the Richmond newspapers—must be abandoned
as hopeless.

This, at any rate, has the merit of simplifying the
matter very much. Only consider how anxiously we
have endeavoured to find out the grievances of the

South which were so intolerable as to justify them, on any principle which has governed mankind at other times, in rushing into a revolution; how many of us have tried every species of conciliation, and have promised guarantees for their future safety, if the people would only return to their duty; how some have gone even further, and presumed to offer up New England as a sacrifice to appease this insatiable Moloch. But it has all been to no purpose. The South has turned a deaf ear to the charmer, "charm he never so wisely." The rebels have in turn been bullied, beaten, starved, and beggared by one party; and flattered, caressed, encouraged, and tempted with fine promises by the other; but to each party they have held precisely the same language—that of stubborn, defiant insult. No; the insane pride of the slaveholder still cherishes the dream of that perfect civilization in which slavery is to be really the corner-stone of the republic, in which every power which can mould the form of government, and every theory which can guide and control its action, shall be due to the pure and unmixed influence of the slave system upon the man and the citizen. Their future association with us would destroy this darling theory, not because we are anti-slavery in our opinions, but simply because nature and our position have unhappily forced us to be non-slaveholding. They glory, therefore, in being aliens and foreigners, and they

present to us the most singular spectacle of a people
saved from utter annihilation, simply because a large
party in the country with which they are at war
refuse to take them at their word.

We cannot, we wish we could, refuse the evi-
dence of our own senses in this matter. The
question is no longer whether we shall restore the
Union upon any terms, or by any possible theory
of reconstruction, not even whether the war is carried on upon principles, and with certain indications
of a policy which we may not all approve, but it
seems to us that it is narrowed down to this,
whether our own permanent peace and security do
not require us to crush effectually a scheme, which
would establish on our borders an independent
sovereignty.

Let us look fairly at the portentous significance
of the project before us, and reflect upon the inevitable consequences to our own safety and peace
if it should be successful. This is no mere senti-
mental nor speculative matter. It has nothing to
do with our pride in preserving the integrity of our
national existence in the eyes of the world, nothing
to do with any mere philanthropic feelings in regard
to the condition of the slaves, but it addresses itself
to our deepest instincts, to considerations connected
with the value and safety of our property, with our
love of peace, and with all our hopes of the future,
as those hopes are bound up in the belief of our

capacity for developing our natural resources. Every
man in the free States who owns a dollar's worth of
property, or who has the smallest belief in the value
of free institutions, is as much interested in the settlement of this matter, as if it were proposed to place
the territory, which the South now claims, under the
absolute sovereignty of England, France, or Russia.
There is no middle ground. It can no longer be
disguised that the rebels have determined to establish, if they can, two separate nations out of the
common territory, and that no concessions we can
make, no securities we can offer, nothing but the
irresistible power of a victorious army can change
their purpose.

This is the issue we have to meet, plain and
unmistakable, and it does really seem as if it had
been forced upon us just at this crisis, by the direct
interposition of Divine Providence, to recall that
united and generous enthusiasm with which this
contest was first entered upon, and to rouse into
efficient action that deep, common, universal instinct
of the American heart—its intense nationality, which
has only been slumbering of late, because it feared
misdirection. In the legitimate influence of this
sentiment is our sure ground of hope. Let us not
forget that in all the angry discussions about the
policy of the war, while the theory of one party may
be called that of conciliation, and that of the other,
coercion, the avowed object of both has been the

same—the restoration of the Union. The Democratic party has hoped against hope, profoundly convinced of the inestimable value of the Union, and fondly believing that a policy of concession would secure its restoration. This is observable in all its public acts, and even in the avowals of those who are supposed by many to entertain very extreme views on the subject of concession. These opinions are only the outgrowth of that common sentiment of American nationality, which is powerful with them in common with men of all parties. That this nation shall be ONE, no matter at what cost of pride or principle, is their inmost desire. No one conspicuous in that party, so far as we know, with a single exception, to which we shall refer hereafter, has ever favoured the scheme of southern independence. On the contrary, Governor Seymour, Mr. Van Buren, or Mr. Charles Ingersoll, are quite as decided on this point as Mr. Lincoln himself. Mr. Ingersoll, in a recent speech, remarkable not less for the sagacity with which he exposes the folly of this dream of southern independence—a theory, as he truly says, tenable only in connection with a perpetual war—than for the frankness with which he predicts the consequences, tells his southern friends, that if they have really made up their minds to persist in such a scheme, that the North, of all parties, must necessarily become a unit against them and their slave system, and that their ultimate ruin must then become inevitable. These are opinions which must sooner or later be forced upon thinking men of all parties, when they are convinced of the hopelessness of conciliating the South; and the alternative is presented, whether we are to protect our own nearest, home interests, by forcing these people to submit at any cost, or whether, on the other hand, we are to allow them to establish themselves in quiet and undisturbed possession of a powerful sovereignty on our borders.

For let us reflect what this project of southern independence really means. To enumerate only some of the more obvious results, it includes, on the part of the North, the abandonment of Chesapeake Bay, with Fortress Monroe, its guardian at its outlet; the possession, by our enemies, of all the forts on the southern coast, including those at Key West, the Tortugas, and Pensacola, by means of which the safety of the whole commerce of the North with the West Indies, South America, and California, would be jeopardized; it requires the secure protection of a frontier of more than fifteen hundred miles in length; it places the navigation of our great rivers, and especially that of the Mississippi, under such control as might be arranged by treaty with a jealous foreign power; and more than all, and perhaps worse than all, it takes away wholly the power of resisting the encroachments of European powers, who, either in alliance with the South, or taking advantage of its hatred against us, would certainly not fail in any future war to attack us in that quarter which these proposed arrangements would render wholly defence-less. If the success of our enemies is to lead to such results, we may be pretty confident that when the matter is fully understood, there will be but one party at the North—the commonest instinct of self-preservation will make us a unit.

Let us look, then, at this subject from a point of view whence it seems to us it has not been suf-ficiently considered. Let us turn our eyes away from the South, and forget for a moment that the war is waged to restore the Union, or to force rebels into submission. Let us look at home, at the North, and ask ourselves, what would be the consequences to *us*, to our peace, security, or prosperity, if we should falter in this great contest. Let us examine the four great pillars, which support the whole edifice of northern prosperity, so far as that pros-perity can be affected by the action of a govern-ment—the free navigation of the rivers,—the secu-rity of our foreign commerce,—unrestricted inland communication and intercourse,—and safety against foreign invasion, and see how long they are likely to remain standing, if this dream of southern inde-pendence is realized.

The very first idea which suggests itself to the mind in connection with the notion of an indepen-dent sovereignty, is that fruitful source of the longest and bloodiest wars on record in modern times, a long and exposed boundary line. We do not know that the project of independence is sufficiently developed to enable us to say where the proposed boundary line is to run; but be it a river or an imaginary line, it must be more than fifteen hundred miles long. If we follow the practice of European nations, a practice the result of necessity, we must, for our own safety, protect the whole of this line by fortresses. Consider, too, the constant daily irritation arising along the whole of this frontier, owing to mutual jealousies, differing custom-house regulations, and more than all, from that prolific source of trouble, the existence of slavery on one side of the line, and its prohibition on the other. There is a strange theory that there is more likely to be mutual respect in the relations of inhabitants of independent nations, than in those of a people who are kept in unwilling subjection to the same rule. We are pointed to the hatred of the Irish to the English, of the Magyars to the Austrians, of the Italians to the Germans; but if we will recall the feelings of the Greeks to the Turks, of the Belgians to the Dutch, of the Portuguese to the Spaniards, or of the Swiss to the Austrians, we shall discover that the cause of this antipathy lies deeper than a dislike to a common government, and must be sought for in the far more radical differences which arise from an irreconcilable hostility of race and religion. History, alas! lends no support to any such theory. It teaches, on the contrary, that "enmity between contending nations is implacable and venomous, just in the same degree as they have previously stood near each other, or as nature intended the relation of good will to exist between them. It is the secret of all civil and religious wars; it is the secret of divided families; it is the explanation of unrelenting hatred between those who were once bosom friends. Our position would be but the repetition of the Peloponnesian war, or of the German Thirty Years' war, with still greater bitterness between us, because it would be far more unnatural." Can we look calmly at these things, and not feel that a war of twenty years' duration, which would at last teach both parties that their only safety lay in Union, would be preferable to evils so intolerable? Can we consent to owe our safety to a triple line of fortresses, like that which protects France from invasion on the side of Germany and Belgium? or rather can we doubt that the North, with any such prospect before it, would become an "indissoluble unit," and strike down, at any cost, and with overwhelming force, those who set up this monstrous pretension?

If it were possible that, from any motive, or from any possible combination of events in the future, we might yield to such a claim, we would not gain, by thus sacrificing our real interests and our honour, even that poor substitute—peace. If we look at the history of modern Europe, and seek for one word to define the character of the wars which have desolated the continent for the last century and a half, we may most properly call them wars for a frontier. All the passions which have driven men to war in the old world, find at last their expression in the desire to obtain a good frontier, a safe protection against the ambition of their neighbours. What, for instance, was the object of the wars in which the Prince of Orange was engaged in the Low Countries, but to secure a barrier for his native country against the power of France? What were the campaigns of Marlborough but efforts to gain possession of the fortresses of Belgium, and thus protect the dominion of the Emperor of Germany in that country against the ambition of the same power? What was Frederick the Great's seizure of Silesia, but a desire to render the frontier of Prussia safe against Austria and Russia? What, in more modern times, was the grand object of the early wars of the French Revolution, but to obtain what they call their natural frontiers, the Rhine, the Alps, and the Pyrenees? What cost Napoleon his first abdication, but his obstinate refusal to give up this very boundary? What, in our own day, has lost Lombardy to Austria, but her persistence in interfering in the Italian Duchies, with a view of rendering her frontier safe against Sardinia? and

what has been the result of the war which grew out
of these pretensions, but to make the French dream
of a frontier of the maritime Alps a reality? In
the old and settled monarchies of Europe, if one
thing could be supposed to be permanently estab-
lished, after so many ages of strife, it might be supposed that that one thing was the boundaries of the
respective states. Yet, notwithstanding all the
wars, and all the treaty stipulations by which diplomatists have fondly believed that these disputes
had been finally adjusted, these boundaries become
as shifting as the sand, when the whirlwind of
human passion bursts forth, and the sword is made
the arbiter of the destiny of nations. The fortresses
which line every frontier on the continent of Europe
are among the most suggestive objects which the
thoughtful student meets with on his travels.
While they tell of religion menaced, of independence preserved, of ambition curbed, they are also
enduring monuments of a truth which lies deep in
human history,—that no nation has ever been willing to trust its safety to the influence of those sen-
timents of good will and mutual respect which are
supposed to arise from free commercial intercourse
and identity of material interests, but has felt secure
only when girded about with the strongest physical
barriers against the violence of human passions.

If then, a boundary line could be agreed upon in
this country, it does not seem practicable to adopt

the European plan of maintaining it, and it would thus be at the mercy of every outbreak of the bordering population. Even if this was escaped, questions connected with it would be constantly arising, and it needs no prophet to predict, that they would be seized upon by any party, or by any ambitious general of ability, (and it is to be supposed that at some future day the American soil may produce such a personage, although certainly it has been uncommonly niggardly hitherto in this respect,) as pretexts to involve the two countries in a general war. There is a vast deal of practical good sense at the bottom of the theory of American nationality,—the instinctive feeling that this country must be one. Its first introduction into American politics was under the auspices of a very wise and eminently practical man, to whose counsels American independence owes perhaps as much as to those of any other one man— Dr. Franklin. It is not generally known, but it is a fact now well vouched for, that at the first meeting of the Commissioners in Paris, to settle upon the terms of the Treaty of 1783, Dr. Franklin proposed that England should cede the whole of Canada to the United States, with a view, as he stated, of preventing the possibility of any future disputes between rival powers on this continent. His anxiety to secure an early peace, and the great victory of Rodney over the Count de Grasse, by which the French fleet in the West Indies was

destroyed, occurring just at this time, probably
deterred him from further urging this project,
which had been a favourite one with him at least
as early as the year 1778. What would have been
our position now, had this grand idea been then
carried into execution?

Another problem closely connected with the
question of boundaries, and, perhaps, even more difficult of practical solution on the theory of southern independence, is the enjoyment of the navigation of the great rivers, which, rising in the
free States, run so long a portion of their course
in the southern territory. It is hardly necessary
to say a word upon the inestimable value of these
great channels of communication to the prosperity
of the ten millions of freemen, who are now asked
to hold so dear a right at the sufferance of those
for whose use, in common with themselves, that
right was originally secured. We may refer to it
merely to remind the reader that the free navigation of the Mississippi river to its mouth, has been
necessarily from the beginning the central idea of
all western progress, as the river itself has been the
main artery along which has flowed hitherto the rich
stream of its happy and prosperous life. Its indis-
pensable value to all western developement was
seen at the earliest period of the history of the government, and strenuous efforts were made to secure
as free a navigation of the river as was consistent

with the possession of the territory through which it
flowed, by the Crown of Spain. By a treaty made
in 1795, a precarious right of navigation and deposit
at New Orleans was obtained, and this was considered at the time as a most important advantage
gained for the interests of the West. Happily for
us, France, who had succeeded to the Spanish dominion of the country, from a jealous fear lest England might wrest this immense territory from her,
thought fit to sell the magnificent prize to us, and
Mr. Jefferson, with far-seeing sagacity, eagerly seized
the opportunity of acquiring it; thus, as Mr. Everett
expresses it, "violating the Constitution, but found-
ing an empire."

From that day to this, the value of this acquisition
has become more and more real and apparent. Into
that magnificent domain, tempted by the boundless
prospect of success of which the free navigation of
the rivers was the surest guaranty, the ceaseless tide
of emigration has poured, bringing with it the varying forms of modern civilization, and a people has
grown up, enterprising, active, intelligent, perse-
vering, blessed with marvellous prosperity, and
happy in the enjoyment of all the arts of peace.
The people of the East have watched the progress
of their western brethren with a wonder and admi-
ration which has been shared by all the world, and
have looked forward with complacency to the period
when these great and prosperous communities, the

free States of the Valley of the Mississippi, developing to the fullest extent all the wonderful resources of their position, should become the centre and stronghold of our characteristic American civilization. Can any one suppose that this powerful race, with such a career before them, can tamely submit to the abandonment of this glorious heritage, or can consent to hold, at the pleasure of a foreign power, that unrestricted commercial intercourse, which has been the foundation of all its past prosperity, as it is the basis of all its hopes for the future. Certainly, to state such a proposition is to demonstrate its absurdity.

The force of these truths is so apparent that it has penetrated even the minds of those, who, in their revolutionary fury, seem to have forgotten the elementary distinctions between right and wrong, and the rebel Congress, we are told, has declared that the navigation of the Mississippi shall be free. In other words, it is proposed, when southern independence is recognised, to substitute for the free, common, unrestricted use of the great river, as now guaranteed by the Constitution of the United States, a treaty with a foreign power, by which the country shall be equally well secured in its enjoyment. Now, in the first place we may ask, in view of the permanent security of the right, where is there any guaranty that a treaty will be regarded as more binding than the provisions of the Constitution itself which, in one sense, is the most solemn of all treaties? What does the proposition amount to, when stripped of the false importance which some persons, who certainly do not get their ideas from history, attach to the notion of a treaty? Simply this, that the country is to hold this great outlet for her productions at the mercy of a foreign power, and that that power thus holding the very keys of her treasury, may starve her into compliance with any claim it may deem proper to make. But it is said, mutual interest and the laws of trade will settle this matter, the obvious material interests of both countries requiring unrestricted commercial intercourse. All this was eminently true when the jealousies and rivalries of different States in regard to the use of the river, had a common umpire in the Federal Government. But alas! this fearful rebellion has shown that when human passions are roused, material interests, like moral laws, are alike unheeded.

Could we afford to trust this precious jewel in the keeping of the weakest and most pacific foreign power in existence? Its possession would infallibly give to any power the control of the destinies of the continent, and what would it be in the hands of that brave and turbulent race, whom Mr. Russell (the correspondent of the *Times*) describes as possessing,—not the wisdom of the serpent, combined with the harmlessness of the dove, but "the simplicity of children, with the ferocity of tigers."

The first essential to all successful commerce, is a sense of security arising from the consciousness of adequate protection in case of need. But what safety could there be to commerce when any line of policy which we might adopt, should be judged by such a population to be hostile? And how long would the voice of justice or moderation be heeded, when a foreign power had at command so formidable an engine for our destruction? No doubt, in the event of a separation, a treaty might be framed by which the erection of forts on the banks of the river might be prohibited; but, of course, such a stipulation would become inoperative the moment war was declared, although that is the only period when any such arrangement would be of the slightest importance to us.

There is another consideration, showing how impossible it would be to secure the free navigation of the great rivers, on the theory of southern independence; and that is, that in such an event, it is manifest that the political necessity for the control of the rivers to the very existence of the proposed government, would outweigh any question of their mere commercial value, great as it unquestionably is. It is not worth while to argue this point, for it must be clear that no government at the South could surrender, or consent to weaken, in any way, so formidable a means of controlling the action of a power-ful neighbour. It would thus appear that the only alternative in this matter lies between the total abandonment of any real and substantial control over it, and a determination that the right shall be secured, as it now is, by the provisions of the Con-stitution. Would it not be better, in view of these things, that we should fight the matter out now, and settle for ever, who are to be the slaves, and who the masters, if that is the only practical alternative? We cannot help feeling that when our people fully consider the proposition to confide the control of the Mississippi river to a foreign power, a project now veiled under the thin and transparent pretext of a guaranty of its free navigation, they are as likely to assent to it, as to return to the practice of paying a tribute to the Dey of Algiers for protec-tion against his own piratical corsairs.

There is a good deal of misapprehension in some minds as to the peculiar sanctity of provisions in public treaties in regard to the free navigation of rivers. It is supposed that there is something exceptional in their character, which gives them a more permanent existence than the other stipula-tions of a treaty. This is so far from being true, that the principles which now govern this matter were introduced into the public law of Europe as late as the year 1814, when the doctrine of the right of the free navigation of the great rivers in

Europe, in time of peace, was first recognised by the Congress of Vienna. It is true that this is the only addition to the law of nations, among the many which were made by that great assemblage of European diplomatists which has survived to our own day; but the reason is, that no general war has arisen on the continent between powers mutually interested in the subject, (except, perhaps, the dispute about the mouths of the Danube, which was one of the causes of the Crimean war,) so as to bring the matter again into discussion. But we may be sure that while Ehrenbreitstein and Cologne command the Rhine, Antwerp the Scheldt, Mantua the Po, Magdeburg the Elbe, and the fortifications of Lintz the Danube, a war between parties mutually interested in the navigation of these great rivers would not terminate without giving decided advantage to that nation whose power, resulting from the strength and position of its fortifications, could control their course. We must not forget that the practical question with us is, not how the right of navigation is to be secured during a time of peace, for then, as with the air we breathe, it is of interest to no one to interfere with its enjoyment; but how far, in time of war, its control might embarrass our operations, or force us into humiliating concessions. The question was settled by the Congress of Vienna, as a matter of general European concern, and the arrangement was guaranteed by all the powers.

This is precisely the position in which the government of the United States stands in regard to the Mississippi and all our great navigable rivers, so far as the right of every citizen of any State to use them as channels of trade, is concerned. It has neither power nor temptation to grant peculiar privileges to any section, and is only desirous of developing, to the fullest extent, their great value for the convenience of all. This is the only substantial guaranty we can ever have for the permanent enjoyment of these great arteries of civilization, and the proposition of a would-be foreign power to allow us to use our own, as its interests or passions may dictate, is a miserable mockery and insult.

If we wish to know what the great West would think of such a scheme, let us listen to its true voice, as it comes to us in the trumpet tones of noble Rosecrans, rousing the very depths of the soul. "We know that such a blessing as peace is not possible while the unjust and arbitrary power of the rebel leaders confronts and threatens us. Crafty as the fox, cruel as the tiger, they cried 'no coercion,' while preparing to strike us. Bully like, they proposed to fight us, because they said they were able to whip five to one; and now, when driven back, they whine out 'no invasion,' and promise us of the West permission to navigate the Mississippi, if we will be 'good boys,' and do as they bid us. Whenever they have the power, they drive before them into the ranks, the southern people, and they would also drive us. Trust them not. Were they able, they would invade and destroy us without mercy. Absolutely assured of these things, I am amazed that any one could think of 'peace on any terms.' He who entertains the sentiment is fit only to be a slave; he who utters it at this time, is, moreover, a traitor to his country, who deserves the scorn and contempt of all honourable men."

The whole theory of the binding force of treaties, which it is proposed to substitute for the control of the Constitution over the varying interests of the country, and the notion which prevails with some, that peace and security are the better maintained by treaty provisions than in any other way, seem to us very singular, very great delusions. They certainly find no support in history. We have only to study the map of Europe for the last century and a half, to discover that general treaties of peace, so far from being any expression of the real interests of the inhabitants of contending nations, represent only the concessions on one side, rendered necessary by the irresistible argument of victory on the other; and that, even in cases where mutual exhaustion would have seemed to counsel mutual concessions, the slightest military advantage, like the sword of Brennus, has been sure to incline the scale. Treaties based on such principles, where the force of the moment, and not the eternal laws of justice and equity, determine, cannot, in the nature of things, last longer than the pressure of that force remains.

How many times has the map of Europe been wholly remodelled since the beginning of the last century, as the result of wars, arising from alleged violations of the most solemn treaties, whose provisions had been guaranteed by all the powers. It is a lamentable fact, that neither prince nor people has ever been restrained, (when either has had the power,) by any provisions of treaties of the most formal kind, from dealing with their neighbours in any way which their interests, or ambition, or love of conquest might prompt. The glory of our own system has been, that these disputes, which are inevitable between populations of differing interests, and which, in other countries, have been made the constant pretext for war, have here been submitted to the jurisdiction of the General Government, under the provisions of the Constitution; and if that Constitution is destined now to perish, stricken down by parricidal hands, the fact that for seventy years it kept the peace between rival and jealous sovereignties, if it did nothing else for the general progress of humanity, will always render it the most remarkable plan of government in human history. Let us reflect a moment upon what we have escaped in this country, merely of the evils of war, by being bound together by a Constitution, and not by treaties. Let us look abroad, at the fearful experience of Europe under a system which it is proposed we shall now adopt, and be thankful for the past, and wise for the future.

No sooner was the treaty of Utrecht signed in 1713, by which all the advantages which had been gained by England, in the campaigns of Marlborough, were given up by Bolingbroke, who, as the event proved, while Minister of Queen Anne, was also the agent of the Pretender and friend of Louis XIV., than intrigues began in various courts of Europe to set aside its provisions. Spain, under the guidance of that most remarkable man, Cardinal Alberoni, although the recognition of Philip as her sovereign was almost the only condition of the treaty likely to remain permanent, became dissatisfied with her abandonment of her Italian possessions, and declared war against the house of Austria, to recover them. This, of course, at once set Europe in a blaze, which was not extinguished until the overwhelming force of the Quadruple Alliance enabled it once more to carve up the continent at the pleasure of its members. Pure exhaustion kept the nations quiet, until Frederick the Great, ambitious to enlarge his territory, not having the fear of treaties before his eyes, and thinking that he had only three women, Catherine of Russia, Maria Theresa, and Madame de Pompadour, to oppose his schemes of conquest, plunged Europe into a war which lasted more than seven

years, and certainly destroyed the lives of more
than a million of men. The result of it all was
that Silesia became a Prussian instead of an Aus-
trian province. So with the famous treaty of Paris
in 1763, after another long war, in which the real
object was doubtless, on the part of England, wholly
to destroy the maritime power of France, new
arrangements were made in regard to the territorial
possessions of the different powers, not only in
Europe, but on this continent, wholly inconsistent
both with the provisions of the treaty of Utrecht
and of that of Aix-la-Chapelle. Passing by the
revolutionary era, and coming down to the period
when legitimacy reigned triumphant, when the
earnest desire, and obvious interest of the various
nations combined to force upon them all the necessity of devising some plan of remodelling Europe,
which would be permanently secure against the
encroachments of dynastic ambition or revolutionary
passions, what, we may ask, has become of the
laborious work of the Congress of Vienna, although
the arrangements then made, with a view of securing a permanent peace, were mutually guaranteed
by all the powers, great and small? Greece torn
from Turkey, Belgium from Holland, Lombardy
from Austria, and the rest of Italy quietly taken
from its recognised princes, and handed over to the
house of Sardinia; the family of Napoleon, with
whom the Congress had declared it would never

treat, and to exclude whom from the throne of
France at any future time, had been the anxious
desire of all who signed the treaty, now firmly rees-
tablished in power—what are all these events, hap-
pening within the last fifty years, but a complete
commentary upon the folly and delusion of the belief,
that any treaties between foreign powers will last a
moment longer than any one of them may have the
inclination and force to break them? Let us think
of these things. Let us be grateful, when we remember that the Constitution alone has secured to
us the blessings of peace in the past; and let us
determine that peace shall be maintained in the
future, as indeed it only can be, by enforcing a universal recognition of its mild and beneficent sway.

We have endeavoured to show the incompatibility
of southern independence with any security to a proposed frontier, or with the enjoyment of the right of
navigation of the great rivers. Let us look for a
moment how our interests would be affected by the
possession of the forts on the southern coast, particu-
larly those at Key West, the Tortugas, and Pensacola. It is impossible to find language more em-
phatic in the expression of an opinion as to the value
of these forts, in a national point of view, than that
employed by Mr. Maury, late a captain in the United
States Navy. This man, with some pretensions to
science, which he employed in a great measure to
debauch public sentiment at the South, by inflaming

it with golden dreams about the commerce of the Amazon and alliances with the great slave empire of Brazil, was ordered by the Secretary of War to present his views on the general subject of national defences. In an elaborate report, dated in August, 1851, he says: "A maritime enemy seizing upon Key West and the Tortugas could land a few heavy guns from his ship, and make it difficult for us to dislodge him; so long as he held that position, so long would he control the commercial mouth of the great Mississippi Valley. In that position he would shut up in the Gulf whatever force inferior to his own we might have there. He would prevent reinforcements sent to relieve it from Boston, New York, and Norfolk, from entering the Gulf. Indeed, in a war with England, the Tortugas and Key West being in her possession, it might be more advisable, instead of sending from our Atlantic dock-yards a fleet to the Gulf, to send it over to the British Islands, *and sound the Irish people as to throwing off their allegiance.*" It was, as is well known, to secure these important positions, commanding the entrance into the Gulf, and the commerce of the Gulf itself, that Florida was purchased from Spain. If such would be the condition of things during actual hostilities, how completely should our policy in time of peace be governed by considerations as to the safety of our foreign commerce with half the world, which these strongholds in the hands of an enemy might com-

pletely destroy. There is no need of statistics here.
The most unobservant is forced to ask, what is to
become of the commerce of our great maritime cities,
and of the thousand interests which are bound up
with it, in such an event? Let us learn wisdom from
the example of other nations in this matter. England, as is well known, at the termination of all the
great wars in Europe, has steadily refused any territorial acquisitions on that continent, preferring the
possession of certain strongholds in different quarters
of the globe, which would enable her to maintain in
every quarter her commercial supremacy, and thus
effectually control the policy of the world where her
own peculiar interests were likely to be affected.
Gibraltar, Corfu, Malta, the Cape of Good Hope,
Aden, Singapore, Hong-Kong, Jamaica, Bermuda,
Halifax, what are these but a standing menace to
other powers, that her commercial supremacy is to be
maintained in all quarters, at all hazards? It is
barely conceivable that any government we might
have at the North, under any future combination of
events, would dare voluntarily to abandon these great
safeguards of our commerce. To such a suggestion,
the only answer could be that of Mr. Pitt to the
Spanish negotiators of the treaty of 1763, who asked
England to give up some trumpery claim about
curing fish on the coast of Newfoundland, and were
told that the minister would not dare to do it, even
if the Spaniards were in possession of the Tower of

London. These positions are of course just as important to the South as they are to us, for without them the South could have no real independence. We hold them now, and while their possession, with that of so many other vital points, convinces every thoughtful man how much real progress we have made in the course which, if persisted in, must sooner or later bring our enemies to reason, we are not likely to forego the present or future advantage which their possession gives us.

Our capacity for successful resistance, in case of a foreign invasion, is a subject closely linked with our material prosperity, and it would be vastly diminished by the establishment of southern independence. All our arrangements for national defence have been made on the assumption of the perpetual Union of the country. To what a condition would we be reduced in our controversies with a foreign maritime power, should such a power be in possession of the forts on the southern coast, and of Fortress Monroe in particular. We may rest assured that the very first step by which a foreign power would attempt to enforce its pretensions, in any future disputes with this country, would be an alliance with the South. Our disunion would then have produced its bitterest fruits, for we should have the sad spectacle of a family strife, in which any gain would fall into the hands of a stranger. The utter inability of the South to maintain herself as

a maritime power, and her most probable enemy
being one of the chief naval powers of the world,
would necessarily force her in the end to throw
herself into the arms of some European nation for
protection and safety.   It does not conflict with
this theory, that the South may be strong enough to
achieve her independence, because the efforts by
which that independence is gained, if it is ever
gained, must necessarily be exceptional, and cannot
be repeated; any government, even that of the
Prince of darkness himself, being preferable, as a
permanent system, to the rule which has existed
there for the last two years.   We, in Pennsylvania,
have a very near interest in this matter.   We cannot forget that on the two occasions in which our
territory has been threatened with invasion by a
foreign power, the enemy approached us through
Chesapeake Bay.   Those who have heedlessly
thought, that for the sake of peace the South might
be permitted to go, taking with it everything below
a certain line, without injury to us, would do well
to remember the battle of Brandywine, the conse-
quent occupation of Philadelphia, and the winter at
Valley Forge—the darkest hour of the Revolution;
nor should they forget that other projected invasion
which we escaped, because its force was stayed by
the victories at North Point and Fort McHenry;
and that both of these invasions were attempted
because the Chesapeake was then, what it is pro-

posed to make it again, by our own act, an open highway for such an enterprise.

We might thus go on enumerating a vast array of exclusively northern interests which would be inevitably stricken down by the establishment of southern independence. But they all cluster round the four main supports of our whole system, which we have examined, and we trust that enough has been said to make it apparent that any hope of a permanent peace, the security of our property, our capacity for developing our natural resources, and our ability to make ourselves strong at home and respected abroad, depend upon our united determination to crush forever any such project. These truths have long appeared so self-evident to us, that we have sought with no little curiosity to discover by what means any northern man proposed to reconcile the obvious conflict of the interests of every one of his own countrymen with this scheme of southern independence. We have never seen the propriety of recognising the South as a foreign power, so far as we can remember, advocated in print by a northern man, except in a recent production of Mr. William B. Reed; and although Mr. Reed concerns himself very little with the peculiar interests of his own countrymen, whom he seems to regard with a strange contempt, yet he does favour recognition as a certain mode of securing a desirable peace. There are many things in this pamphlet of which we cannot trust

3

ourselves to speak as we feel, and we refer to it now
merely to show the unsatisfactory mode in which
Mr. Reed disposes of the all-important questions of
boundaries and the right of navigation.*   In regard
to the first, the only mode of settlement proposed,
"the only conceivable mode," is to allow each State
to settle the matter for itself.   Kentucky and Mary-
land are to be permitted to secede without any
reference to their constitutional relations to ourselves, supposing that political entity, called the
United States, still to survive; or to the injury
which their action might inflict upon our most
obvious material interests, supposing their territory,
in the event of a dissolution, essential to the safety
and security of the North.   So in regard to the
other; the navigation of the rivers is to be left with
the "States concerned;" that is, a foreign country
controlling their course and outlet, we are to be
satisfied that in peace and war that control will
always be exercised with the most exact and jealous
regard to our rights and interests.   If we do not
assent to this peaceful mode of yielding up our most
vital interests, then we are threatened with an

---

* We differ from Mr. Reed in many things, but we cordially join him in
his protest against dragging the private life and personal motives of our
opponents into the arena of bitter party strife.   Many, in these unhappy
days, have reached conclusions directly opposite to those of Mr. Reed,
through a path of duty beset with sore trials; and their remembrance of
the sacrifices they have made of life-long friendships, and even of tenderer
ties, is too fresh to permit them to judge, with indiscriminate harshness,
the motives of those who may not agree with them.

aggressive war, to compel us to do so; a war the horror of which is to be aggravated by a fierce strife among ourselves, one party being supposed to be in arms for the purpose of purchasing the poor privilege of joining the Confederacy, into whose blessed fellowship we are now told we may not come even as slaves. What is all this, but a most extraordinary and characteristic commentary upon the peaceful mode of settling the business? Everything the South wants, as a matter of taste or of interest, must be yielded, or we must give it up at the sword's point; but we are to strike neither for the Constitution, which is set at naught, nor for the preservation of those interests of which it is the only guaranty, when they are imperilled by the arrogant pretensions of the rebellion. Mr. Reed is certainly too accomplished a student of history, not to know that such vital questions as those of boundaries, and the right of navigation, were never settled in this way. The appeal has been made to force, and force only can decide it, and that decision, when the people of the North are not misled and deluded by these vain promises of peace, cannot for a moment be doubted.

Mr. Reed points us to Mr. Pitt's opposition to the war of the Revolution. It is certainly not a little amusing to find the man who had so intense a hatred of the claim of any nation to govern itself, as to arm the whole of Europe against France, and to carry on a war from the prompt-

ings of that hatred, which no one now denies
was "accursed, wicked, barbarous, cruel," and the
rest,—it is singular, we say, to find such a man
held up as the opponent of the American war,
upon any principle which can find favour with us.
The truth is, Mr. Pitt was seeking for office in
1781, and during the French Revolution he was
wielding despotic power. In what striking contrast
is this miserable shifting of political principle with
the last grand scene of the public life of Mr. Pitt's
illustrious father, the great Earl of Chatham! He
had been the early friend of the colonists, and the
earnest advocate of their claims, so long as the advo-
cacy of those claims was consistent with the allegiance which he owed his sovereign. He came to
the House of Lords, for the last time, a dying man.
"Yet never," says the historian, "was seen a figure
of more dignity; he appeared like a being of a supe-
rior species." He took his hand from his crutch,
and raised it, lifting his eyes towards heaven, and
said: " I thank God that I have been enabled
to come here this day. I am old and infirm, have
one foot,—more than one foot—in the grave. I am
risen from my bed, to stand up in the cause of my
country." He gave the whole history of the American war, detailing the measures to which he had
objected, and the evil consequences which he had
foretold. He then expressed his indignation at the
idea, which he had heard had gone forth, of yield-

ing up the sovereignty of America; he called for vigorous and prompt exertion; he rejoiced that he was still alive to lift up his voice against the first dismemberment of this ancient and most noble monarchy. Well may the historian add: "Who does not feel that, were the choice before him, he would rather live that one triumphant hour of pain and suffering, than through the longest career of thriving and successful selfishness."*

The practical conclusions to which all the considerations we have urged, point, are, that the rebel theory of independence necessarily makes certain claims which are inconsistent not only with our security, but with our national existence, with the safety of our homes, and the enjoyment of our property, that these claims are practically exclusive in their character, and that as any compromise or arrangement, such as is provided by the Constitution, is wholly rejected by one party, and as we cannot depend upon the force of treaties permanently to guarantee a satisfactory settlement, nothing is left but an appeal to force, to decide who shall control the great elementary conditions of national life on this continent. The appeal being thus made, the nature and character of the settlement depend entirely upon the measure of the success of our arms. This, as we have shown by

* Lord Chatham's example illustrates another matter: While he manfully supported a war which he had earnestly sought to prevent, he did not hesitate to denounce most bitterly one of the means used by the Ministry to prosecute that war, namely, the employment of Indians as allies.

historical examples, is the experience of all nations.
It betrays a gross ignorance of human nature to
suppose that sitting down quietly, and offering
terms of peace, which are prompted by a desire for
conciliation, will ever cause the South to yield her
haughty pretensions to independence.   All such
overtures are looked upon as so many evidences of
weakness, and as was to be expected, their authors
have been treated with contempt and derision.   The
South is under no such delusion, as some of our good
people here, as to a pacific settlement.   They know
they are striving to gain what is just as important to
us, as it is to them, and in such a contest they know
that the sword must be the only arbiter.   If, then,
these interests which we have discussed, are so essential to the North, and if they cannot co-exist with
southern independence, then we must fight it out
until some hope of a reasonable settlement rises out
of the fortunes of war.   The result of the war in the
end, if we remain united, is of course a foregone
conclusion, and with the hope of preserving that
unity of action which must result, sooner or later, in
an irresistible power, we have endeavoured to show
how the common interest of every northern man is
bound up in the result.

May we venture, in an earnest spirit of conciliation, to make a few suggestions to each of the great
parties which now divide the country, and whose
concord in this matter is so essential?

The position of the Democratic party at this crisis is one of great responsibility. So far as we can now judge, the practical solution of the matter is likely to fall into their hands, they probably holding the majority in the next Congress. While we have full confidence in their anxiety to preserve our nationality, our fear is, that in their desire for peace, they may be led into concessions which may weaken us, and not accomplish the object for which they seek. They should never forget, in all their measures, that already we hold positions in the southern territory which, with the blockade of their coasts, the possession of the forts, and of the outlet of the Mississippi, must practically settle the matter in the end in our favour, even if we confine ourselves to maintaining these positions without advancing a single step further. We keep what we take, at any rate, whereas the aggressive war policy of the South has been, so far, a miserable failure. Now, it is hardly to be supposed, that the Democratic party could go before the people of the North, and ask their consent to the abandonment of such advantages. They are not likely to forget, that in a very dark hour of the war of 1812, happily for them as supporters of that war, news came that England, who had expressed great anxiety for peace, proposed as the basis of a treaty, to prohibit us from fortifying our northern frontier, and from keeping a naval force on the great lakes, while a right of navigation of the Mississippi should

be secured to her, and that these monstrous pretensions, when they become known, united the whole
people in favour of the further prosecution of a war,
which had been quite as bitterly opposed as that in
which we are now engaged. The time has not yet
come for the application of the peaceful theories of
settlement by which the Democratic party hope to
heal our present troubles. That time will assuredly
come, if they are not too impatient; and if they
show to the South an united front, teaching them by
that sternest of all masters—the fate of war—to
whose inexorable logic we must all in the end bow,
that their choice is between safety within the protection of the Constitution, and, at the best, the bar-
ren sceptre of a worthless, because short-lived and
merely nominal independence.

With the same anxious desire for conciliation,
and with equal frankness, we propose to make a few
suggestions to the party now in power. Is it not
manifest that our hopes for success in this war
depend practically, not upon our waging it in such a
way as to produce a conviction that its real object
is to remove an evil, which, however great, is not
likely to rouse any general enthusiasm at the North
for its destruction, but rather upon our finding some
policy, no matter what it is for the moment, upon
which we can all be united? Was not this policy
most unexpectedly revealed to us after the fall of
Sumter, and did not the unity then happily estab-

lished, receive the unanimous recognition of the present Congress in July 1861? Have we not become weaker just in proportion as we have wandered from the great, broad, catholic, policy then announced? Whatever may be the effect of the policy of the proposed emancipation of the negroes upon the strength of the military resources of the South, and we do not believe that it will be favour- able to us, is not one thing certain, that at the North, this policy as a military measure, (and this is of course, the only ground upon which it can be justified,) has produced most disastrous results? With a view to the restoration of the Union, have we any right to regard those in rebellion as aliens and foreigners, because they choose to call themselves such? While there is no instance in modern his- tory in which a formidable insurrection has been suppressed save by force, is there an instance in which the crushing power of military success has not been accompanied by the fullest promise of amnesty, a complete recognition of the rights, civil and religious, of the inhabitants, and a guaranty of the absolute security of the property of those who laid down their arms? We venture to make these suggestions because we feel that the real obstacles to the successful termination of this war are to be found, not so much in the means of defence pos- sessed by the rebels, as in the divisions which the adoption of these new and doubtful theories intro-

duce among us.   The only test of any measure, just
now, it seems to us, should be, how will it affect our
military operations? and where any policy, however
promising it may look as a theory, is new and
untried, and must inevitably divide us, then it should
be abandoned.

There are many loyal but desponding people who,
impatient of final results, forget to look at the progress we have already made towards the attainment
of our object.   Our enemies understand this better
than ourselves, and the *Richmond Examiner* only
echoes the opinion of unprejudiced observers abroad,
when it says that another such year of progress, and
the Confederacy is doomed.   "'The Yankees keep
all they take,"—this is the true expression of our
real strength, and their relative weakness.   Look
for a moment at the position of the South, as com-
pared with that of France in the invasion of 1814.
Her enemies were mighty in number, but their
armies were made up of men who had been constantly defeated by the French in the battles of the
previous twenty years.   She was surrounded by sea
and land, as the South is, but the invaders had not
the advantages we possess, of holding, in the heart
of the enemy's country, most important strategical
points, and the great lines of communication; yet
did any one hope that even the mighty genius of
Napoleon, never more conspicuous than it was in
that campaign, could save France from final defeat

against such odds? The result in the end, we cannot repeat it too often, is a simple question of endurance; although if we were to settle to-morrow with the South, on the basis of the *uti possidetis*—keeping only what we now hold—their independence as a nation would be a very unsubstantial shadow. Look once more at the English experience. From January 1807, to July 1809, eighteen months, English expeditions of importance met with failures, more or less disastrous, at Constantinople, at Rosetta, at the Island of Capri, at Buenos Ayres, and at Walcheren. They lost the battle of Talavera, and Sir John Moore's army was driven out of Spain. The only successes gained by the English in Europe during these eighteen months, either military or naval, were the capture of Copenhagen, Lord Cochrane's brilliant victory over the French fleet in Basque Roads, and two battles in Portugal. But the first of these events made Denmark and Russia open enemies to England, and Wellington's victories were rendered valueless by the subsequent retreat from Talavera.*

---

* The want of elasticity in the American character is certainly very remarkable. At one time, according to the newspapers, every movement was a victory; and at another, when these "organs of public opinion" were in a different mood, events which have proved really our most important successes, were looked upon either as indecisive battles or as failures. There are some people even now, who are not willing to believe that Antietam, which completely destroyed the unbounded hopes of the rebels in the success of an aggressive war, was a victory. We are obliged to learn from intercepted despatches, that the battle of Perryville, which at one blow delivered the whole of Kentucky, was a disaster to the South; and we find even the General-in-Chief telegraphing to Rosecrans that the

There are some who fear that the disorganizing
spirit which has manifested itself in certain parts of
the country, may in the end penetrate to the army,
and there produce disastrous results. We confess
that we have too high an opinion of the intelligence
of our soldiers, and too profound a conviction of the
deliberate earnestness with which most of them have
entered upon this contest, to entertain any such
apprehensions.   Brave men have an instinctive
hatred of traitors and cowards, and are quite pre-
pared both for the fire of the open enemy, and for
that of the more insidious foe "in the rear."   Our
soldiers are fighting for an idea,—the sacred idea of
country, and are not to be drawn aside from pressing
onwards to the end, because some of the means
adopted by the government may be distasteful to
them.   Certainly the most ungracious aspect which
the disloyal opposition to the government presents,
finding fault with everything that is done, because
some great mistakes may have been made, is the

rebel accounts confirm his own report of his victory.   How differently
they manage such things in France! Here is part of a song which was
written and sung with "rapturous applause," in one of the darkest hours
of her history.

> "Le coq Français est le coq de la gloire,
> Par le revers il n'est point abattu,
> Il chante fort s'il gagne la victoire,
> Encor plus fort quand il est bien battu.
> Le coq Français est le coq de la gloire
> Toujours chanter est sa grande vertu;
> Est il imprudent, est il sage,
> C'est ce qu'on ne peut définir,
> *Mais qui ne perd jamais courage,*
> *Se rend maitre de l'avenir.*"

implied censure it casts upon our armies in the field. With singular unanimity, we have urged our noble defenders to rush to the rescue of the country in peril, and they have gone forth, men of all parties, and of every shade of opinion, to take our places in the great battle. They at least have "fought the good fight," with a single eye to the glory and honour of their country. It is impossible to honour these heroic men too highly, or to cherish them too tenderly. While there is a spark of patriotism or gratitude remaining in our national life,—while there is a sentiment of national glory or national honour left to preserve us from that political decay which our senseless discord must breed,—while there is a remembrance of the dauntless valour and noble self-sacrifice which characterise the army,—while there is a tender reverence for the memory of the martyrs who have fallen, we shall shrink from doing or saying anything which may weaken the faith of our soldiers in the holy cause in which they peril their lives. If the time ever comes when political passions shall so blind us, as to tempt us to obtain our ends by efforts to demoralize our armies, God Almighty help us! for we shall then have richly deserved the fate which He has reserved for the nations visited in His anger.

There are some whose scruples it is impossible not to respect, who are lukewarm in the support of the war, because they think they see in certain acts of violence done to those principles of constitutional restraint which lie at the basis of our system, a tendency which, if carried out, would destroy our barriers against despotic power. To such men, the restoration of the Union, or the subjugation of the South, would be dearly purchased by the sacrifice of the safeguards of our own political rights. We think all such fears exaggerated, still it cannot be doubted that they exercise a pernicious influence. No one who has been brought up to revere the great principles of constitutional liberty can regard with favour what is called "military necessity," or *raison d' état*, still it is clear, that there are rare contingencies in which, like the law of self-preservation, it must be invoked and irregularly applied. No nation has ever gone to war without violating in some essential manner the well-settled rules which govern it in times of peace, and the dictatorship of the Romans, and the suspension of the writ of *habeas corpus*, are only different ways of recognising the same great necessity. One of the great evils of war, is that it requires for its prosecution such a concentration of power in the hands of the Executive that there is very great danger of abuse in its exercise. After all, however, we must never forget that in this unhappy condition of things our choice is reduced to a choice of evils. Shall we submit to a temporary despotism now, in order that we may be saved from one tenfold more fearful in the future?

It is satisfactory to find that history does not show any permanent ill effects upon the attachment of

a people to free institutions, as the result of war.
On the contrary, the activity and progress in every
department which characterize the present generation in Europe, can readily be traced to the
effects, direct or remote, of the wars which grew
out of the events of the French Revolution. Yet,
in England, good men and wise men, despaired
not only of their country, but of the great cause
of civilization and liberty. In that country, "in
the early part of the war with revolutionary France,
if a man was known to be a Reformer, he was
constantly in danger of being arrested, and even
the confidence of domestic life was violated; no
opponent of the government was safe under his own
roof against the tales of eavesdroppers and the gos-
sip of servants; not only were the most strenuous
attempts made to silence the press, but the book-
sellers were so constantly prosecuted, that they did
not dare to publish a work if its author was obnox-
ious to the Court. Indeed, whoever opposed the
government, was proclaimed an enemy to his country. Every popular leader was in personal danger,
and every popular assemblage was dispersed either by
threats or by military execution." "And yet," adds
Mr. Buckle, from whose work we have taken this
gloomy picture, "such is the force of liberal opinions,
when they have once taken root in the popular
mind, that notwithstanding all this, it was found
impossible to stifle them, or even to prevent their

increase.   In a few years that generation began to
pass away, a better one succeeded in its place, and
the system of tyranny fell to the ground.   And thus
it is that in all countries which are even tolerably
free, every system must fall if it opposes the march
of opinions, and gives shelter to maxims and institutions repugnant to the spirit of the age.   In this
sort of contest the ultimate result is never doubtful.
The vigour of public opinion is not exposed to casu-
alties; it is unaffected by the laws of mortality; it
does not flourish to-day and decline to-morrow; and
so far from depending upon the lives of individual
men, it is governed by large general causes, which
are in short periods scarcely seen, but on a compa-
rison of long periods are found to outweigh all
other considerations."

Let us then, who have offered on the altar of our
country, our treasure and the blood of our brethren,
not hesitate even to make a temporary sacrifice of
our constitutional rights, if the success of the great
cause in which we are engaged renders so cruel a
necessity apparent.   For with success comes peace,
not a peace which would prove a short-lived and
deceptive truce, but a peace which would revive in
all their former vigour the guarantees of personal
rights, and which, even if it did not restore the
Union as it was, would at least secure to us those
conditions of safety which are as the very life-
blood of our existence.

www.ingramcontent.com/pod-product-compliance
Lightning Source LLC
Chambersburg PA
CBHW021546270326
41930CB00008B/1383